DATE DUE

Series Editor: Rosalind Kerven

Printed in Hong Kong

00 99 98 97 96
10 9 8 7 6 5 4 3 2 1

Library of Congress Cataloging-in-Publication Data

Kerven, Rosalind.
    Kintu's mistake / retold by Rosalind Kerven;
    illustrated by Matilda Harrison.
        p.   cm. — (Myths and legends)
        Summary: Kintu, the first man on earth, passes the tests required
    to marry the first woman but fails to heed her warning and
    consequently brings death into the world.
        ISBN 1-57572-015-9 (lib.)
        [1. Ganda (African people)—Folklore. 2. Folklore—Uganda.]
    3. Fire—Folklore.] I. Harrison, Matilda, ill. II. Title
    III. Series: Myths and legends (Crystal Lake, Ill.)
    PZ8.1.K45Kj   1996
        398'.2'096761'01—dc20
        [E]   95-38243

Acknowledgments
Title page and border illustration, pp. 2–3: Hilary Evans;
map, p. 2: Dave Bowyer;
photographs, p. 3: Robert Harding

Kintu's
Mistake

Retold by Rosalind Kerven
Illustrated by Matilda Harrison
Series Editor: Rosalind Kerven

About the Ganda People

This story comes from the Ganda people
who live in East Africa.
In the old days, their land was ruled by
a powerful king.
It is a rich, fertile place that grows good crops
of bananas, coffee, and cotton.
In 1966, the Ganda region
became part of the bigger
country of Uganda.

Map of Uganda

AFRICA

UGANDA

UGANDA

ZAÏRE

Ganda
Region

KENYA

Lake
Victoria

TANZANIA

Most Ganda
people are
Christians now,
but long ago
they had their
own religion.
Their stories told
of gods, nature-
spirits, ancestors,
and kings.

This story is about the first man and woman.

▲ Today many Ganda people still live in the countryside
where they have small family farms.
Others live in modern towns.

The first man who ever lived on Earth
was Kintu.
Don't ask me where he came from.
One day he just appeared out of nowhere!
All he owned was a cow,
so he had nothing to eat,
only milk to drink.

The first woman who ever lived on Earth
was Nambi.
Her father was the god Gulu.
She and her brothers came down to Earth
from the Sky.
As soon as she arrived, she saw Kintu.

Nambi and Kintu started talking.
They liked each other very much.
They fell in love and wanted to get married,
but Nambi's brothers tried to stop them.
"That Kintu seems very strange and foolish," they said.
"The only food he has is milk.
He doesn't seem like a real man."

Nambi's brothers took Kintu's cow away.
Poor Kintu!
Without that cow he was starving.
He couldn't find anything to eat
except the bark of trees.
But kind Nambi rescued him.
"Come with me up to the Sky," she said.
"I want you to meet my father."

So Kintu followed Nambi up to the Sky.
He was amazed at what he saw there!
There were people everywhere—
big villages full of fine houses
and many, many chickens, sheep, cattle,
goats, bananas, and other food.

Nambi's father, Gulu, was waiting for them.
The old god peered closely at Kintu.
He couldn't decide what to think of him.
"So you want to marry my daughter?" he said.
"Well young fellow, I'm going to test you first,
to find out if you're good enough."

Gulu got his servants to build a big house.
Inside they put a thousand bananas,
a thousand hunks of beef,
and a thousand pots of beer.
They pushed Kintu inside and locked the door.
"You have to eat and drink everything," they said,
"otherwise, you will never see Nambi again!"

10

Kintu's heart sank.
He could never get through all this!
But just when he was going to give up,
a great pit suddenly opened in the floor!
Quickly, Kintu threw all the food and beer into it—
and then the pit closed itself up tightly again.
"I've finished!" he shouted.

Gulu was very impressed to see that
everything had disappeared.
"Well, well," he said, "I'll let you marry Nambi—
but first you must get your own cow back.
It is here somewhere, lost among my own cattle."
Kintu's heart sank again.
Gulu had twenty thousand cows—
and they all looked exactly the same as his!

12

He was about to give up
when a wasp came buzzing around his ear.
"Zzz," said the wasp. "Watch me, my friend.
I shall fly to your own cow."
The wasp buzzed off, here and there, everywhere.
At last it landed on a cow's horn.
"That's mine!" shouted Kintu, running up to it.

Gulu was even more impressed this time.
"You're cleverer than I thought," he said.
"You can even beat me at my own tricks.
Come along then, let's fix up the wedding."

The next day they held a great wedding feast,
with lots of music and dancing.
Afterwards Gulu presented the bride and groom
with many gifts.
Among them were seeds to grow on their own farm
and a fat chicken.

Then Gulu kissed his daughter goodbye
and sent them both down to live on Earth.
"Have a safe journey," said Gulu.
"But remember this—
whatever happens, even if you
have forgotten something,
do not turn back."

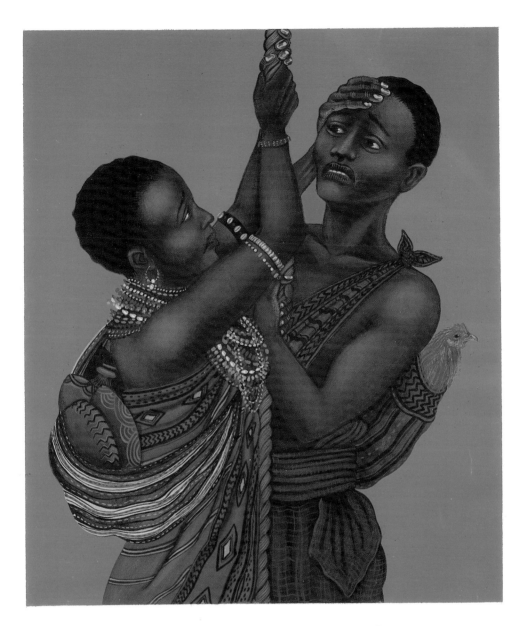

Well, Kintu and Nambi were half-way home
when Kintu suddenly stopped.
"Oh no," he cried, "I'm such a fool!
I've forgotten the corn to feed the chicken.
It will starve without it.
I'll have to go back to the Sky to get it."

"You can't!" cried Nambi.
"Remember what my father said—
something terrible will happen if you turn back."
"But think of that poor hungry chicken," said Kintu.
"Don't worry, I'll be perfectly all right."
And before Nambi could stop him, he was gone.

Back in the Sky, Kintu hurried into Gulu's house
and picked up the forgotten bag of corn.
On his way out, he met a stranger.
"Hello," said the young man, "I'm Nambi's
other brother.
May I come down to Earth with you?"
"Of course," said Kintu.
"All my wife's family are welcome in my house."

When Nambi saw her lost brother following Kintu
her eyes grew wide with anger.
"What's the matter?" asked Kintu.
Nambi took him aside.
"You should never have brought him here,"
she whispered.
"He's a dangerous man—for his name is Death!"

20

But it was too late.
They were stuck with him now.
Kintu built a house
and all three of them lived there together.
At first things went fairly well.
But one day they had a big argument.

Death was furious with Kintu and Nambi.
"Listen," he screeched at them,
"you are getting old.
Soon I shall be able to kill you!"
Nambi and Kintu stared at him in horror.
"Then there will be no people on Earth,"
sneered Death.

22

Kintu rushed straight to the Sky
and asked Gulu for help.
But the old god shook his head and said,
"I can't save you two from dying, I'm afraid.
You should have listened to Nambi's warning.
However, go home and talk to her.
She will know how to keep people living on Earth."

23

So Kintu went back to his wife.
"We must have some children," she smiled.
"That way, even though you and I will die,
there will be people on Earth after us."
So that's what they did.
And still today, people keep on having children.
That's why you're here—
all because of Kintu's mistake!